I0797697

Online Etiquette

Phyllis Cornwall
and John Willis

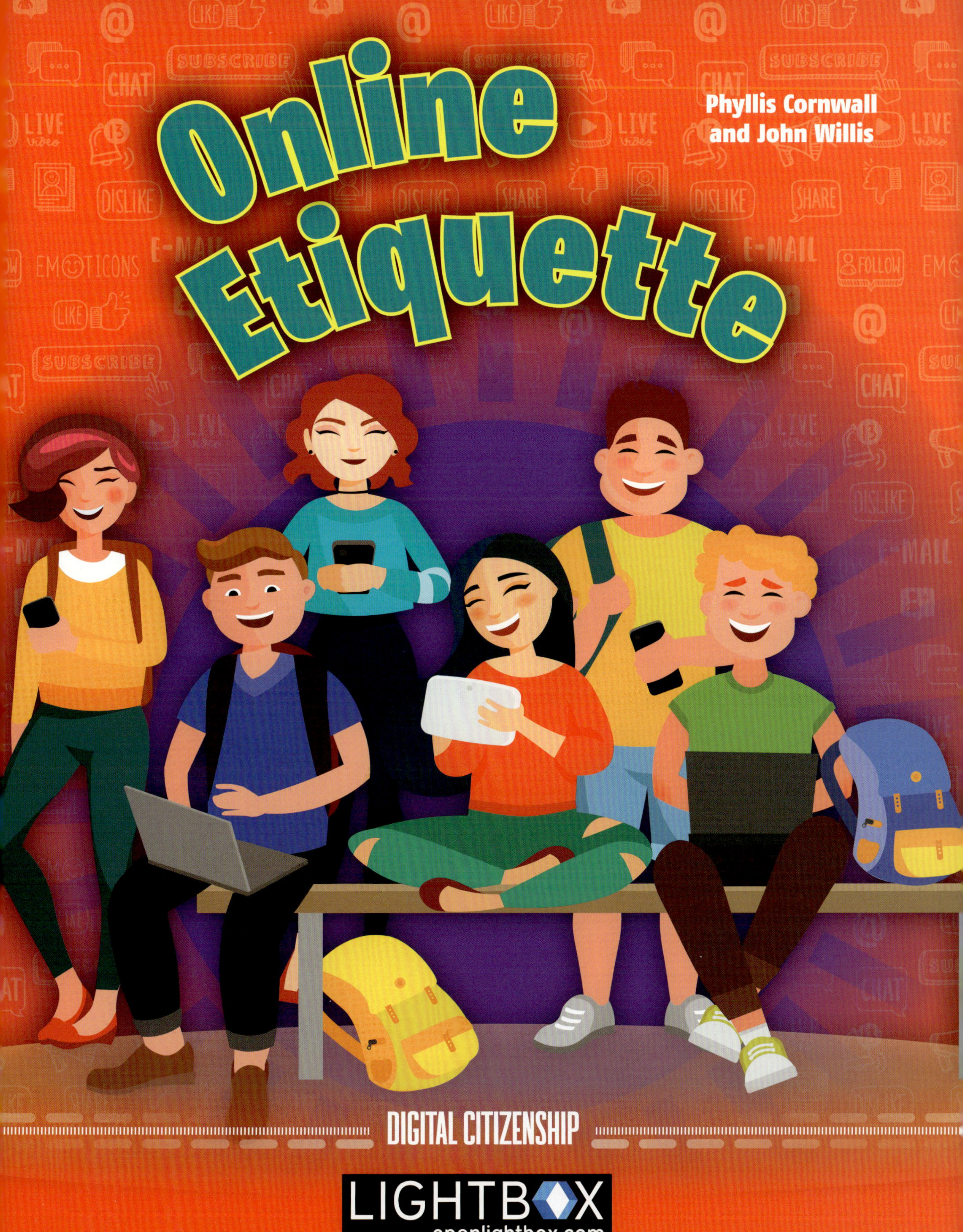

DIGITAL CITIZENSHIP

LIGHTBOX
openlightbox.com

Go to **www.openlightbox.com** and enter this book's unique code.

ACCESS CODE

LBXZ3346

Lightbox is an all-inclusive digital solution for the teaching and learning of curriculum topics in an original, groundbreaking way. Lightbox is based on National Curriculum Standards.

LIGHTBOX SUPPLEMENTARY RESOURCES

SHARE Share titles within your Learning Management System (LMS) or Library Circulation System

CURRICULUM Find national and state curriculum correlations

CITATION Create bibliographical references following the Chicago Manual of Style

STANDARD FEATURES OF LIGHTBOX

AUDIO High-quality narration using text-to-speech system

ACTIVITIES Printable PDFs that can be emailed and graded

SLIDESHOWS Pictorial overviews of key concepts

VIDEOS Embedded high-definition video clips

WEBLINKS Curated links to external, child-safe resources

TRANSPARENCIES Step-by-step layering of maps, diagrams, charts, and timelines

INTERACTIVE MAPS Interactive maps and aerial satellite imagery

QUIZZES Ten multiple-choice questions that are automatically graded and emailed for teacher assessment

KEY WORDS Matching key concepts to their definitions

This title is part of our Lightbox digital subscription

Lightbox Grades 3–5 Subscription
ISBN 978-1-5105-5424-5

Access hundreds of Lightbox titles with our digital subscription. Sign up for a **FREE** subscription trial at **www.openlightbox.com/trial**

Online Etiquette

Contents

1 Chapter One

Minding Your Manners Online

Have you heard people say the word "**etiquette**"? They are talking about good manners.

Wiping messes on your sleeve is bad etiquette.

Etiquette is using good and polite behavior. Sometimes, rules are being followed. However, etiquette is more than rules. Good table manners are part of etiquette. Do you slurp your drink? That is not good etiquette. You are not breaking any rules, but people will think you are not very polite.

Do you throw trash on the floor? That is not good etiquette, either. Schools have rules about cleaning up trash.

The word **"etiquette" was first used** in **1737**.

In 1962, **First Lady Eleanor Roosevelt published** the ***Book of Common Sense Etiquette***.

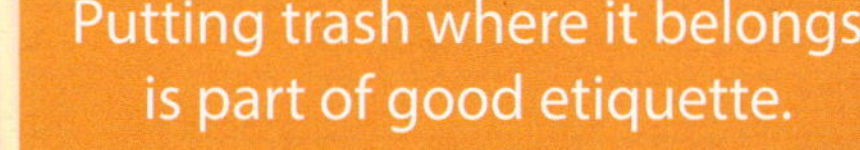

Putting trash where it belongs is part of good etiquette.

Some forms of etiquette, such as speaking respectfully, are important both in person and online.

Sometimes there are manners, and sometimes there are rules. Both are part of etiquette. Using etiquette shows you are respectful of others.

Using etiquette **online** is important, too. Online etiquette is showing respect for others. It makes using the internet safer and more fun.

Is etiquette the same everywhere? Draw a line down the middle of a piece of paper. You now have two columns. At the top of one column, write "My House." Label the other column "A Friend's House." List five things that are considered good manners under each location. Are some manners the same? Are some different? Why is that so?

On a new piece of paper, write "Online Etiquette." List five things you think are good online manners. Compare this list to the lists from the last activity. Which manners are the same? Which are different?

History of Online Etiquette

More than 2,500 years ago
The earliest known texts about etiquette are written in Egypt.

Mid-1970s
The company Xerox gives employees a behavior guide for electronic mail. It is one of the first online etiquette guides.

1982
The word "netiquette," combining "net" and "etiquette," is first used.

1990
Early internet etiquette includes avoiding adding music to web pages to help computers load them more easily.

1998
The internet becomes more widespread and easier for many people to use.

2020
The COVID-19 pandemic causes online etiquette to become more important as many people begin working online from home.

Mapping Online Etiquette

London, United Kingdom, 2014

A study by an international research firm shows that about 28 percent of Americans have directed rude online activity at people they do not know.

Paris, France, 2019

The Organisation for Economic Co-operation and Development (OECD), a group with members including the United States, notes the importance of teaching online etiquette to children.

2 Chapter Two

Online Etiquette: Your Words

Privacy means wanting to keep something to yourself. You may not want to share your thoughts or words. You do not want other people to hear them.

Thinking about something is always private. No one knows what you are thinking. However, words can be written on a piece of paper. That might not be private. Say you gave a friend a note, and she loses it. Your note might be found. Someone else might read it. Your note had been private. Now it is not.

Anyone can read your thoughts if you write them down.

Most things on the internet are public. They can be seen by people around the world.

The same thing can happen online. You might **post** words online. Your words might be seen by many people. They might be copied. They could be sent to people you do not even know. You may think places online are private, but writing on the internet is public. You might have shared your words with people you trust. Your words can still become public.

Suppose you sent a picture to a friend online. The picture shows you doing something silly. Your friend thinks the picture is very funny. He sends it to other people. But you did not say that he could do that. Now, other people can see the photo. It might embarrass you. It might even cause you to get into trouble. Always ask yourself these questions before posting something online:

1. Would I say this to my friend out loud?
2. Could someone print what I wrote and show it to his or her parents?
3. Would my parents or teacher like my words?
4. How might the person reading this feel?

Always ask for someone's permission before posting any images of them online.

Try This

What is the difference between public and private? Below is a list of places and things. Can you tell which are public and which are private?

1. The library
2. A neighbor's yard
3. A newspaper
4. Your journal

ANSWERS: 1. public, 2. private, 3. public, 4. private

3 Chapter Three

Online Etiquette: Blogging

Following someone's **blog** can be fun. You can learn a great deal. Blogs are like online diaries or journals. The writer posts his or her thoughts. They might be about events, places, or people. Most blogs let visitors leave comments. Practice good online etiquette when you are visiting a blog.

Do you want to post a comment on a blog? Here is a good rule to follow. Cannot think of anything nice to say? Then do not say anything at all. You do not have to agree with everything you read, but there is always a respectful way to say something.

There are more than 600 million blogs on the internet.

Be friendly to people online just like you would if you met them in person. It is important to remember that there is another person behind the screen.

Your comments should never be rude or hurtful. Say you went to someone's home. Would you say bad things about the furniture there? Visiting a blog is like being a guest in someone's home. Treat the writer and his or her guests with respect.

What if you make a mistake? You might post the same comment more than once. Delete the extra comment if you can. If not, apologize to the blog writer by email. You could also post your apology with another comment.

Things you read on a blog might make you angry. They might upset you. Stop visiting that blog. Do not waste your time posting comments. Move on and find a new blog. There are many fun blogs on the internet. You will easily find another one.

An adult, such as a teacher or parent, can help you find an age-appropriate blog about any topic you find interesting.

Try This

Suppose you had your own blog. You want your visitors to follow good etiquette. Can you list five tips of good etiquette for your blog visitors? What about for the blog writer? What five rules of etiquette should you follow?

Etiquette I Should Follow:

Etiquette My Readers Should Follow:

4 Chapter Four

Online Bullying

Bullies pick on people. A bully might push someone down on the playground. He or she might say something mean. That can hurt someone's feelings. Did you know there are also bullies on the internet? A **cyberbully** uses the internet to pick on others.

How do you know if you are being cyberbullied? You might get **threatening** emails from someone you do not know. There might be mean posts on your school online bulletin board. These might say bad things about you.

Cyberbullies can be found anywhere online where people are able to communicate with each other.

Cyberbullies can be just as hurtful as the bullies people meet in person.

Cyberbullying is not harmless fun. People who are cyberbullied often become very sad. They may be scared. They may avoid their friends. They may not do their favorite activities.

If you are unsure about a text message, wait and re-read it before sending it. You may no longer want to send it.

Be careful that you do not cyberbully. Do not send mean emails. Do not send threatening text messages. Avoid posting pictures that could embarrass someone. Do not pretend to be someone else. Never trick someone into giving you personal information. Never send someone's personal information to others. Use good online etiquette. Treat others the way you want to be treated.

Try This

Knowing what to do about a cyberbully is important. How much do you know? Below is a list of possible actions. Which actions listed below should you do? Which should you NOT do?

1. Tell a parent, teacher, or trusted adult.
2. Respond to bullying messages.
3. Save bullying messages. Do not delete them.
4. Trust your feelings. If something feels wrong, tell someone.

ANSWERS: 1. yes; always tell an adult as soon as it happens, 2. no; never respond to a cyberbully, 3. yes; saved messages can provide proof of cyberbullying to the police or other authorities, 4. yes; if something feels wrong, it probably is.

Quiz

1
Which internet-related word was first used in 1982?

2
What does a cyberbully use the internet to do?

3
Who can read your thoughts if you write them down?

4
What does using etiquette show?

5
What can visitors leave on most blogs?

6
What percent of Americans have directed rude online activity at people they do not know?

7
Where were the first known texts about etiquette written?

8
When was the word "etiquette" first used?

9
How many blogs are on the internet?

10
What should you do if things on a blog make you angry?

Answers: 1. Netiquette **2.** Pick on others **3.** Anyone **4.** That you are respectful of others **5.** Comments **6.** 28 **7.** Egypt **8.** 1737 **9.** More than 600 million **10.** Stop visiting it

Key Words

blog: a website that is a personal, online journal with entries from its author

cyberbully: someone who uses the internet to threaten, pick on, or spread rumors about others

etiquette: rules for good or polite behavior

online: connected to other computers through the internet

post: to put any type of message on a website, which includes writing an email

privacy: keeping others from knowing your thoughts or words

threatening: mean or scary

Index

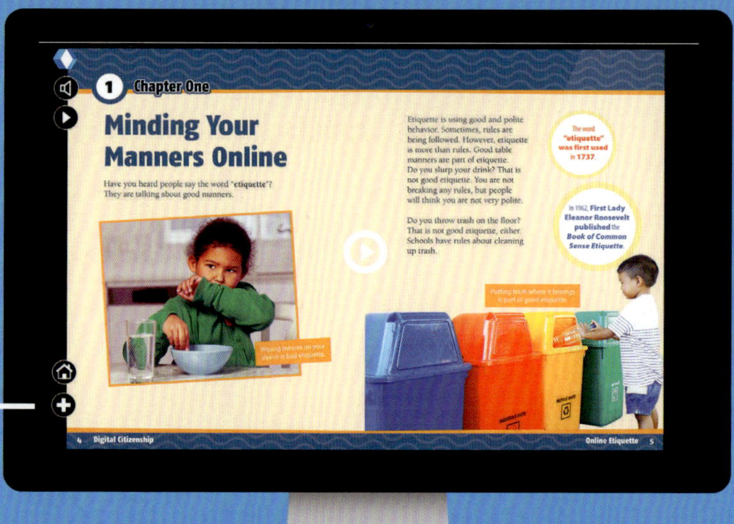

SUPPLEMENTARY RESOURCES

Click on the plus icon found in the bottom left corner of each spread to open additional teacher resources.

- Download and print the book's quizzes and activities
- Access curriculum correlations
- Explore additional web applications that enhance the Lightbox experience

LIGHTBOX DIGITAL TITLES
Packed full of integrated media

VIDEOS

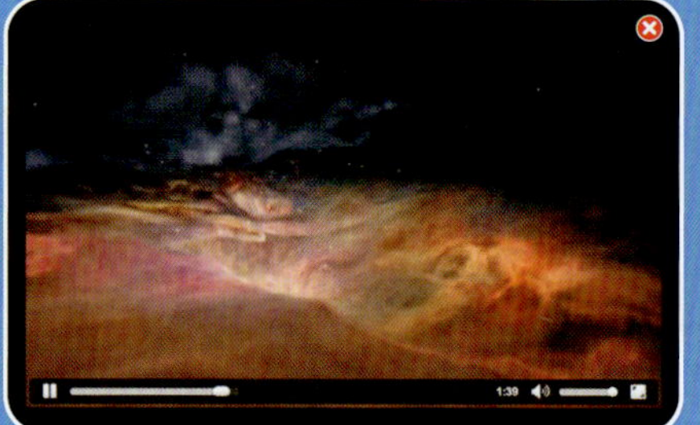

INTERACTIVE MAPS

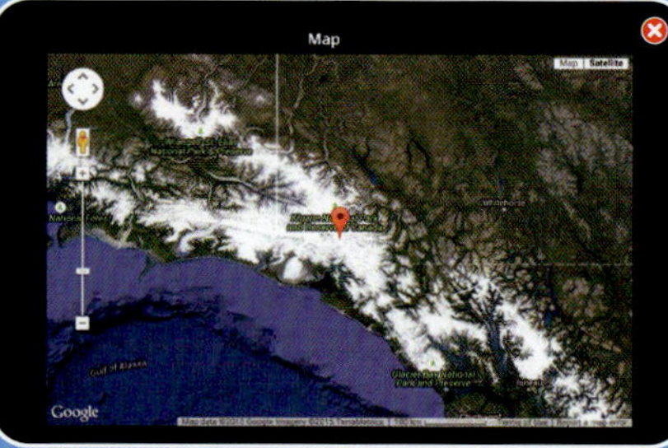

WEBLINKS

SLIDESHOWS

QUIZZES

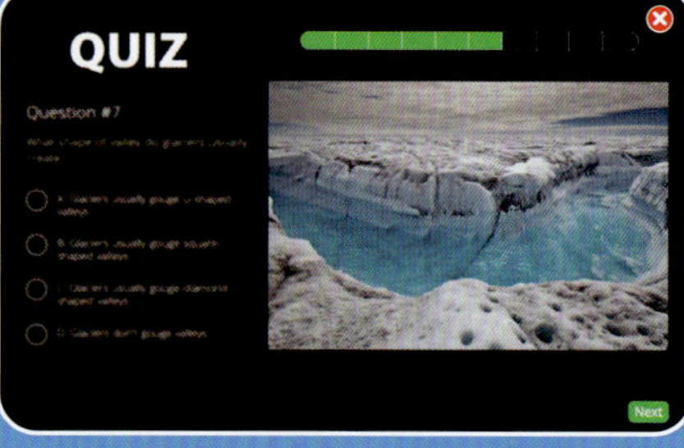

OPTIMIZED FOR

- ✓ TABLETS
- ✓ WHITEBOARDS
- ✓ COMPUTERS
- ✓ AND MUCH MORE!

Published by Lightbox Learning
276 5th Avenue
Suite 704 #917
New York, NY 10001
Website: www.openlightbox.com

First published by Cherry Lake Publishing in 2012

Library of Congress Control Number: 2021939471

ISBN 978-1-5105-5574-7 (hardcover)
ISBN 978-1-5105-5575-4 (multi-user eBook)

Printed in Guangzhou, China
1 2 3 4 5 6 7 8 9 0 25 24 23 22 21

082021
111020

Project Coordinator John Willis
Designer Jean Faye Marie Rodriguez

Photo Credits
Every reasonable effort has been made to trace ownership and to obtain permission to reprint copyright material. The publisher would be pleased to have any errors or omissions brought to its attention so that they may be corrected in subsequent printings.

The publisher acknowledges Getty Images as its primary image supplier for this title.